THE NATIVE AMERICANS

INDIANS OF THE SOUTHWEST

TRADITIONS, HISTORY, LEGENDS, AND LIFE

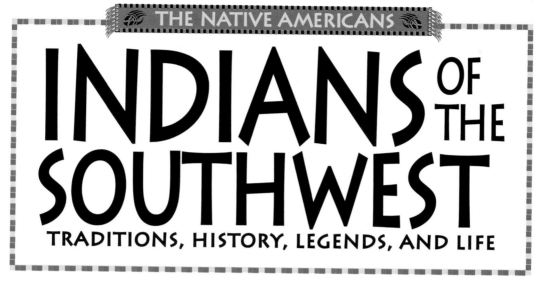

THE NATIVE AMERICANS

INDIANS OF THE SOUTHWEST

TRADITIONS, HISTORY, LEGENDS, AND LIFE

LISA SITA

COURAGE BOOKS

AN IMPRINT OF RUNNING PRESS
PHILADELPHIA • LONDON

Published in the United States in 1997
by Courage Books, an imprint of
Running Press Book Publishers.

Printed in the United Kingdom by Butler & Tanner Limited

9 8 7 6 5 4 3 2 1

Digit on the right indicates the number of this printing.

ISBN 0-7624-0070-6

Library of Congress Cataloging-in-Publication Number 96-69252

THE NATIVE AMERICANS
INDIANS OF THE SOUTHWEST
was prepared and produced by
Michael Friedman Publishing Group, Inc.
15 West 26th Street
New York, New York 10010

Editor: Susan Lauzau
Art Director: Lynne Yeamans
Photography Editors: Colleen A. Branigan and Kathryn Culley

Color separations by Ocean Graphic International Company Ltd.

Published by Courage Books,
an imprint of Running Press Publishers
125 South Twenty-second Street
Philadelphia, Pennsylvania 19103-4399

Contents

INTRODUCTION
The First Americans

By the time Christopher Columbus landed in the New World, it was actually a very old world. Although scientists who study ancient cultures disagree about exactly when the first people arrived in North America, there is general agreement that it was more than eleven thousand years ago. We know this because archaeologists have discovered stone spear points near the remains of hunted mammoths—mammoths that have been extinct for about eleven thousand years!

After their arrival in North America, the first Americans gradually spread across the continent. Each group of people adapted to the climate and conditions of the area where they lived, developing different cultures and different languages. By the time Europeans arrived, about five hundred years ago, the peoples of North America already had a long and varied history.

In this book we'll explore the rich heritage of some of the cultures that flourished in the American Southwest long before the arrival of the Spanish in 1540. These early Americans are most likely the ancestors of the Native peoples living in the Southwest at the time Europeans began to settle the region. You'll learn how the early peoples of the Southwest survived in their harsh environment, finding and growing food, building homes, and raising families. As you read about these ancient cliff dwellers and Pueblo peoples, you'll begin to appreciate the long and extraordinary history of America.

LEARNING ABOUT THE PAST

How do we know as much as we do about the customs and traditions of Native Americans living before the arrival of Europeans? To answer this question, we must look to three kinds of sources.

One source is the archaeological record. Archaeologists study the things that were made and used by early peoples. These objects, which can be anything from tools to buildings, offer many valuable clues about the lifeways of early peoples.

A second source of information is the oral tradition of Native Americans living today. The oral tradtion is a way of passing on information from generation to generation by word of mouth. According to many Native Americans today, certain customs and traditions, especially spiritual traditions, have ancient roots. Native Americans are able to practice them today because these customs and traditions have been handed down to them from their ancestors through the oral tradition.

The written accounts of early European explorers are yet another source of information. When Europeans first arrived in the Americas, they wrote records describing the lifestyles and ceremonies of the peoples they encountered, people who had not yet been influenced by European traditions.

All of these sources together help researchers gain a better understanding of life in North America before European settlers arrived.

🌿 **ABOVE:** THIS EIGHT-HUNDRED-YEAR-OLD CLAY WHISTLE WAS DISCOVERED BY ARCHAEOLOGISTS AT PECOS NATIONAL MONUMENT, NEW MEXICO.
LEFT: MANY NATIVE AMERICANS LIVING TODAY CONTINUE TO PASS DOWN THE STORIES AND CUSTOMS OF THEIR ANCESTORS.

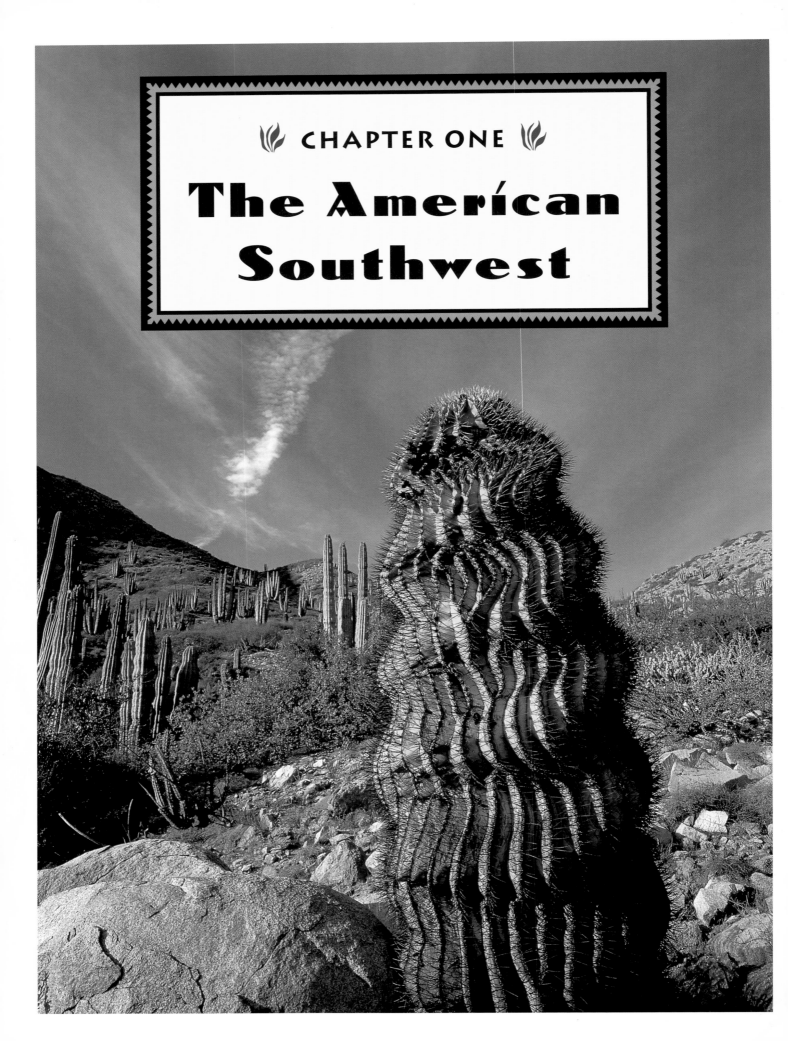

CHAPTER ONE

The American Southwest

🌿 A Varied Land

Before we can understand a people, we must first understand the environment in which they lived. The southwestern United States is a dramatic and beautiful place. Its varied landscape stretches across the states of Arizona, New Mexico, southeast Utah, southwest Colorado, and part of western Texas. It is home to many species of animals and plants.

In the northern region of the Southwest are some of the most magnificent natural land formations in the world, including the famed Grand Canyon. In this region the Colorado River and its tributaries wind through deep canyons, high plateaus, and wide mesas. The land of mid-Arizona and western New Mexico is a place of mountains and valleys thick with forests of pine, juniper, and piñon. The southernmost portion of the Southwest is desert land scattered with sagebrush and cacti. Rivers branch through this area, including the Gila and Salt rivers in southern Arizona. Farther east, the Rio Grande flows through the entire state of New Mexico.

In spite of its beauty, the Southwest is a harsh environment. Very hot days turn into frigid nights until the sun returns the next day in a cycle of extreme heat and cold. The country is generally dry with little rainfall throughout the year. When the rains do come, they often bring flash floods that dry up soon afterward, quickly absorbed into the parched ground. In the winter, blizzards blow across the land, making travel close to impossible. Although living in this environment brings many difficult challenges, the Southwest has been the ancestral home of Native peoples for thousands of years. The ruins of their villages still stand in this majestic land.

🌿 The Southwest landscape features many different species of plants and animals, including the giant barrel cactus (opposite) and the Rocky Mountain juniper (above).

THE SOUTHWEST

The map below shows the many pueblos still in existence today.

Arizona:

The Hopi villages = Including Old Oraibi, Bacavi, Shongopovi, Shipaulovi, Mishongnovi, Sichomovi, Hano, Walpi.

New Mexico:

Desert Pueblos = Zuni, Acoma, Laguna.

River Pueblos = Isleta, Sandia, San Felipe, Santa Ana, Santo Domingo, Cochiti, Zia, Jemez, Tesuque, Nambe, Pojoaque, Santa Clara, San Ildefonso, San Juan, Picuris, Taos.

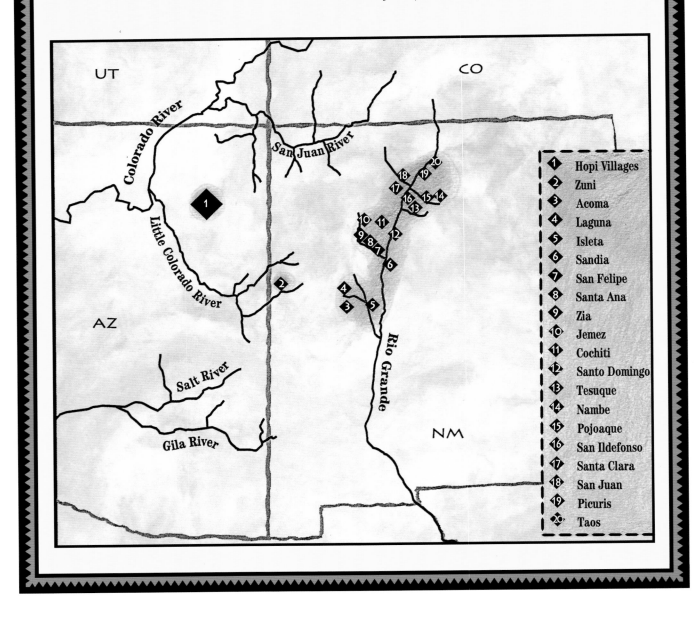

1	Hopi Villages
2	Zuni
3	Acoma
4	Laguna
5	Isleta
6	Sandia
7	San Felipe
8	Santa Ana
9	Zia
10	Jemez
11	Cochiti
12	Santo Domingo
13	Tesuque
14	Nambe
15	Pojoaque
16	San Ildefonso
17	Santa Clara
18	San Juan
19	Picuris
20	Taos

Peoples of the Southwest

Among the earliest peoples to live in the Southwest were three cultures known today as the Hohokam, the Mogollon, and the Anasazi. These cultures developed in different parts of the Southwest during roughly the same time period, from about A.D. 200 to 1450. The Hohokam lived in the desert region of southern Arizona. Their descendants are believed to be the modern peoples of this region, including the Tohono O'odham (or Papago), Pima, Yaqui, Mojave, and Maricopa.

The Mogollon lived in the mountainous area ranging from the borders of Arizona and New Mexico into northern Mexico, while the Anasazi lived among the canyons and mesas near what is today called the Four Corners region—the area where New Mexico, Arizona, Colorado, and Utah meet. The Anasazi are also known as the Cliff Dwellers because they built their homes in cliffs and overhangs and on mesas. The descendants of the Mogollon and the Anasazi are the Pueblo peoples of today.

Each of these various groups developed unique cultures suited to the kinds of southwestern environments in which they lived. The Pueblo peoples were among the first to depend on agriculture for their food supply, and

A YOUNG BOY FROM SAN ILDEFONSO DRESSED IN COLORFUL DANCE REGALIA

so they were one of the first to live in permanent settlements. (The word *pueblo,* a Spanish word meaning "town," was used by the Spanish after first encountering

ANIMALS AND PLANTS OF THE SOUTHWEST

The following are only a few of the various types of plant and animal life found in the Southwest.

Mammals
- *Mountain Lion*
- *Peccary*
- *Coyote*
- *Jackrabbit*
- *Mule Deer*
- *Squirrel*

LEFT: MOUNTAIN LION

ABOVE: PECCARIES

Birds and Reptiles
- *Roadrunner*
- *Owl*
- *Hawk*
- *Wren*
- *Lizard*
- *Snake*

ABOVE: SAW-WHET OWL CHICKS

LEFT: RED-TAILED HAWK

Trees and Other Plants
- *Cactus*
- *Sagebrush*
- *Yucca*
- *Snakeweed*
- *Piñon*
- *Juniper*

LEFT: BEAVERTAIL CACTUS

ABOVE: SNAKEWEED

Above:

Jackrabbit

Below:

Mule deer

Above:

Coyote pup

Above:

Ground

squirrel

Right:

Cactus

wren

Above: Rattlesnake

Left:

Cones from

the piñon

tree

Left:

Utah

juniper

these villages of multistory buildings. *Pueblo* refers to the people as well as to the towns they inhabited.) Some pueblos were built along the Rio Grande and are known as river pueblos. The modern pueblos of San Ildefonso, Cochiti, and Taos are just a few of the river pueblos in existence today. Other pueblos were built in the drier region west of the river. Surviving pueblos include Zuni, Acoma, and Laguna in New Mexico, and the villages of the Hopi in Arizona (while the Hopi do live in pueblos, their settlements are generally referred to as villages).

SNAKETOWN: A HOHOKAM VILLAGE

Much of what we know about Hohokam culture has come from discoveries at a site called Snaketown. (Snaketown got its name from the great number of snakes found there in the nineteenth century.) This village is one of the oldest Hohokam sites and was occupied for more than one thousand years. There is still much more to be learned from Snaketown, which is now protected so that archaeologists may work on it in the future.

ABOVE: THIS HOHOKAM POT WAS DISCOVERED AT SNAKETOWN. ARCHAEOLOGISTS THINK THE PAINTED FIGURES DEPICTED ARE DOING A CEREMONIAL DANCE.

DWELLINGS IN MODERN-DAY TAOS PUEBLO. THESE TRADITIONAL HOMES RETAIN THE BEAUTY OF EARLY PUEBLOS.

OPPOSITE: A double ladder leads to a kiva in Acoma Pueblo. The kiva was an important and sacred place for the Anasazi. **BELOW**: A view of Acoma Pueblo from the valley floor

Many of today's pueblos are centuries old. Two of the oldest settlements in North America, which have been lived in continually since they were first built more than one thousand years ago, are Acoma Pueblo and the Hopi village of Old Oraibi. Acoma, Old Oraibi, and other early pueblos were built using sandstone, clay, and other natural materials. With their warm colors, the villages blended nicely into the surrounding landscape. This was in keeping with the Pueblo belief that humans should live in harmony with the land and all living things on it. To the Pueblo peoples, the land has always been sacred, and they have always believed that in order to survive, humans must maintain a balance between the physical world and the spiritual world.

ANCIENT NEIGHBORS

Although the Anasazi, Mogollon, and Hohokam were the three main cultures to thrive in the ancient Southwest, they were by no means the only ones. One group, the Sinagua, occupied the area of what is today Flagstaff, Arizona. They lived in pit houses, grew corn, and actively exchanged goods and ideas with other peoples of the Southwest.

Another group, the Salado, lived close to the Anasazi, Mogollon, and Hohokam. Their location allowed them to share many ideas with their neighbors. The Salado also farmed, built cobblestone pueblos, wove cotton cloth, and made distinctive pottery with black and white designs on a red background.

A third culture, the Fremont, occupied western Utah and the northwest corner of Colorado. Although they grew corn, the Fremont relied more on hunting and gathering than did the Anasazi. They lived in pit houses, made gray pottery in a variety of shapes, and are well known today for the detailed pictographs, or rock paintings, they left behind.

What became of the Sinagua, Salado, and Fremont cultures is still uncertain. Some archaeologists believe that droughts and other climate changes forced them to migrate out of the area or perhaps join with neighboring groups. Others propose that they left because of warfare, epidemics, or overuse of their natural resources. Still others believe that they remained in the area and are the ancestors of some present-day southwestern peoples.

LEFT: THIS NECKLACE OF SHELL AND STONE BEADS WAS MADE BY PEOPLES OF THE SINAGUA CULTURE CENTURIES AGO. **BELOW:** ANCIENT STRUCTURES BUILT BY THE PEOPLES OF THE SALADO CULTURE

The ancient cliff houses built by the Anasazi almost a thousand years ago are among the best-preserved ruins found in the Southwest today. More than twenty-five thousand sites have been identified in New Mexico alone. Archaeologists have revealed that the early peoples of the Southwest had complex cultures with sophisticated technologies that allowed them to irrigate the dry land for farming, to establish villages of carefully constructed buildings, to develop an elaborate religious system, and to create intricately woven baskets, fine pottery, beautiful jewelry, and other items that are today considered works of art. These traditions were main-

ᘛ Anasazi dwellings at Mesa Verde National Park, Colorado. Many Anasazi pueblos were built in rocky alcoves that had eroded into the cliffsides. Here they were shielded from the weather and protected from attack.

tained by the later pueblo dwellers, whose modern descendants rank today among the world's finest artists, and who continue to maintain their ancient cycle of rituals and ceremonies while successfully farming the arid land of the Southwest.

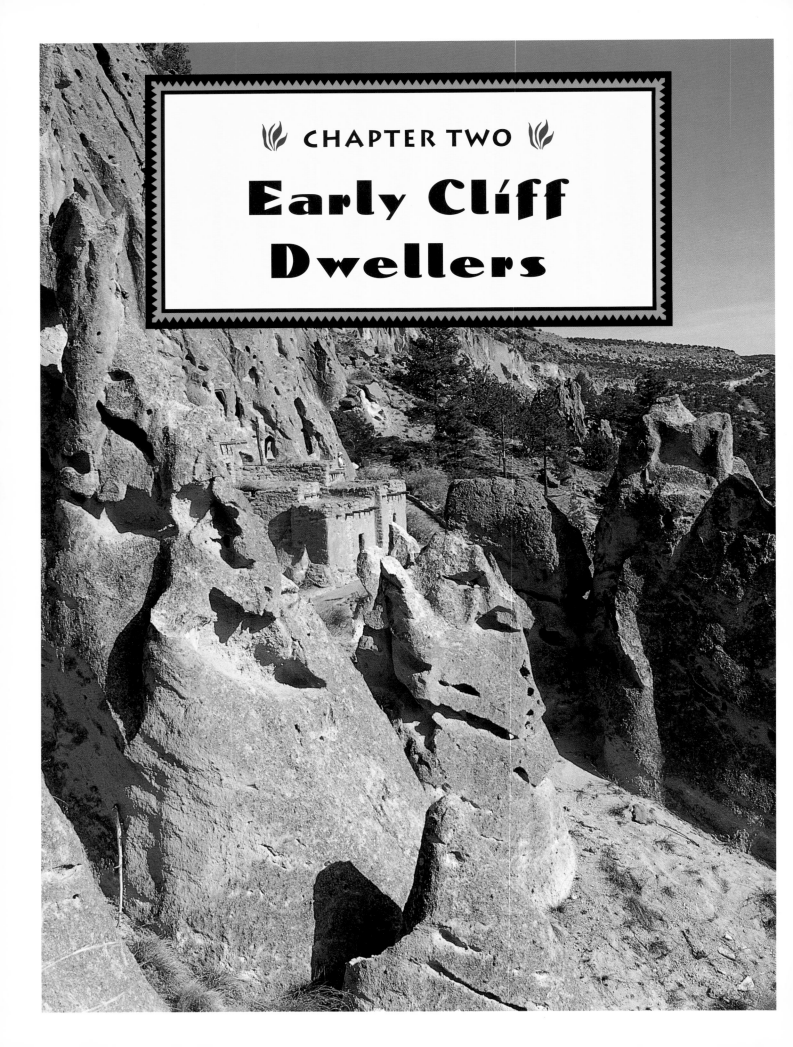

CHAPTER TWO

Early Cliff Dwellers

The Ancient Ones

Humans were living in the Southwest at least nine thousand years ago and maybe as many as twenty thousand years ago. The earliest groups were probably small family bands that roamed the land in search of food. They hunted small game like rabbits, lizards, and birds and gathered grass seeds, piñon nuts, berries, and other wild plant foods. These early people found shelter in caves and rock hangings and made clothing and blankets of rabbit fur. They also made tools and utensils of stone, bone, and wood, including milling stones for grinding seeds and nuts.

Then, between about 1000 and 500 B.C., something important happened: some of the people of the Southwest began to grow corn, also called maize, in areas where the land and climate would permit it. (Corn growing originated in Mexico, but eventually this practice spread throughout the Americas.) Although the new farmers continued some hunting and gathering, with this new development they no longer needed to wander as far or as often for food. They began to settle permanently, although other groups who continued the hunting and gathering way of life sometimes raided the settled peoples for their crops.

These early farmers of the Southwest also began to cultivate beans and squash. At first, they probably moved up to the mountains in spring, at the beginning of the planting season. There the whole family would help to clear the field and plant crops, which took about a month. Once the plants started to grow, the family would move away so that they could gather wild plants, but would return in early autumn to harvest their corn and other crops.

The Mogollon

By around 300 B.C. these early farmers were settling into villages close to their farming plots. The houses they made, called "pit houses," were partially dug into the ground and were usually round. A framework of wood, brush, and earth covered the pit. Pit houses had entrance ramps, and storage pits and hearths were dug into the floor. By about 100 B.C. these ancient people had learned how to make pottery, a skill they probably learned from peoples farther south in Mexico. This way of life was the beginning of what archaeologists would later call the Mogollon culture. (The name *Mogollon* comes from the Mogollon Mountains of this region,

OPPOSITE: ANASAZI DWELLINGS AT BANDELIER NATIONAL MONUMENT, NEW MEXICO. ABOVE: A CLAY POT MADE BY THE MOGOLLON ABOUT NINE HUNDRED YEARS AGO

ANCIENT CITIES

Listed below are some of the sites where ancient cities of the Southwest once stood and which are now open to the visiting public.

HOHOKAM

Pueblo Grande Ruin, Arizona

Casa Grande Ruins National Monument, Arizona

MOGOLLON

Gila Cliff Dwellings National Monument, New Mexico

ANASAZI

Navajo National Monument, Arizona

Salmon Ruins, Colorado

Aztec Ruins National Monument, Colorado

Mesa Verde National Park, Colorado

Canyon de Chelly National Monument, New Mexico

Chaco Culture National Historical Park, New Mexico

Pecos National Monument, New Mexico

Bandelier National Monument, New Mexico

HOHOKAM DWELLINGS AT CASA GRANDE RUINS, ARIZONA

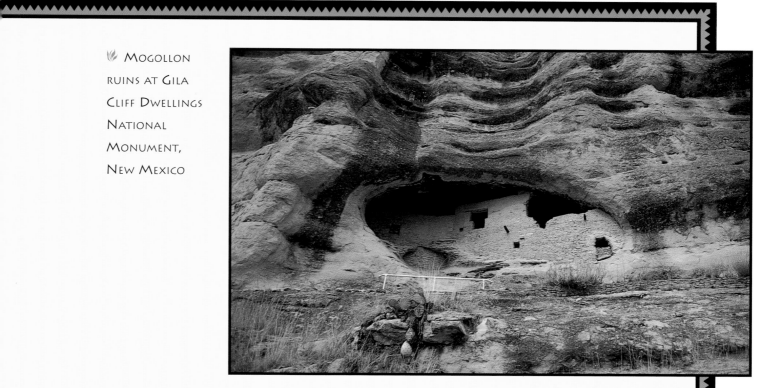

🌿 Mogollon ruins at Gila Cliff Dwellings National Monument, New Mexico

🌿 Anasazi dwellings at the foot of Canyon de Chelly National Monument, New Mexico

which were named for an early Spanish governor.) The Mogollon people are well known today for their pottery. Especially valued are the black-on-white painted bowls produced by the Mimbres culture, a branch of the Mogollon. These bowls were painted with figures of animals, people, and supernatural beings. Many were buried with the dead, usually with holes punched in their bottoms. Archaeologists believe the holes have ritual significance, perhaps to "kill" the bowl or to release its spirit into the next world.

The Hohokam

A few hundred miles west of the Mogollon lived the Hohokam. Hohokam culture began to emerge about two thousand years ago in the blistering desert of southern Arizona. (The name Hohokam comes from the Pima language and means "those who have gone" or "the vanished ones.") In the beginning, the Hohokam lived much like the Mogollon: they farmed the land, built pit houses, and made pottery. Later, however, they made certain changes in their way of life that were probably influenced by the civilizations of Mexico.

One change came when the Hohokam began to irrigate their fields. They dug irrigation ditches that channeled water from the Gila and Salt rivers to their fields. An ingenious system of dams and levees allowed farmers to control the amount of water their crops received. In time, these ditches developed into a network of canals spanning as many as thirty miles (48km) and sometimes more. One network spread over 150 miles (240km). This steady supply of water ensured a larger harvest. Since the Hohokam could produce more food, their settlements grew larger. Some villages may have had only a few families living in them, but others had several hundred people.

A prominent feature of Hohokam life was trading. They sent their goods (such as cotton, turquoise, and salt) south into Mexico, and in return they got items like seashells, exotic birds, and copper bells. Expanded trading brought resources from afar to Hohokam artisans. They further developed their pottery-making techniques, crafted ornaments of turquoise and shell, made stone vessels and mirrors of pyrite, made etchings in shell that may be the first in the world, wove fine cloth, and sculpted lifelike clay figurines.

The Hohokam also built large and impressive ball courts. These ball courts were elevated, with sides made of sunbaked clay, and the largest of them provided enough space for five hundred people to watch the event. While nobody knows exactly how the Hohokam played their ball games or what other ceremonies might have taken place on the courts, archaeologists think

ANCIENT ROCK ART

Figures of animals, supernatural beings, and human hands can be found on rocks and canyon walls across the Southwest. Some of them were painted using natural pigments made from crushed minerals. These are called "pictographs." Others were carved into the rock using stone tools. These are called "petroglyphs." These paintings and carvings, some of them much more than a thousand years old, were made by the Hohokam, Mogollon, and Anasazi centuries ago. Archaeologists believe the figures were associated with the peoples' religious beliefs, and because the figures were created using different artistic styles, archaeologists can figure out which of the three cultures made them.

ABOVE LEFT: A PICTOGRAPH OF A HUMAN-LIKE FIGURE WITH A BOW AND ARROW FROM CANYONLANDS NATIONAL PARK, UTAH. **ABOVE RIGHT:** IN "THE CLIFF DWELLERS," ARTIST E.I. COUSE DEPICTS A SOUTHWESTERN MAN CARVING A PETROGLYPH CENTURIES AGO WHILE TWO BOYS, PERHAPS HIS SONS OR NEPHEWS, WATCH. **LEFT:** A PETROGLYPH FROM MESA VERDE NATIONAL PARK, SHOWING HUMANLIKE FIGURES, HANDS, ANIMALS, AND GEOMETRIC SHAPES

that ball games served as opportunities for different Hohokam villages to get together. This made trade among the communities easier and also may have been a way for men and women to find suitable marriage partners.

In addition to ball courts and, of course, their pit houses, the Hohokam built large, earthen mounds. These sloping, man-made hills were constructed of dirt and trash, similar to today's landfills. Archaeologists believe that the flat tops of these mounds may have been used as platforms for ceremonial dances.

During the same period that the Hohokam were building their distinctive mounds, they also began cremating their dead. This practice became an important part of Hohokam culture, and the remains of cremation burials have been found in excavated ball courts, though the meaning of these discoveries is still unclear.

🌿 The Anasazi

North of the Mogollon and the Hohokam lived the Anasazi. (The name Anasazi comes from the Navajo language and means "ancient ones" or "enemy ancestors.") About two thousand years ago, while the Hohokam and Mogollon were farming and making pottery, the Anasazi were in their Basket Maker period (about A.D. 1 to 400). They had not yet begun to farm, still relying on hunting and gathering for food. In addition to making tools of stone, bone, and wood, they did fine basketry work, making coiled baskets, sandals, and other items of woven plant material.

🌿 **TOP:** THESE BEAUTIFULLY CRAFTED ITEMS, MADE AND USED BY THE ANASAZI IN THEIR DAILY LIVES, WERE DISCOVERED AT MESA VERDE. **ABOVE:** A FLINT KNIFE MADE BY THE ANASAZI. **OPPOSITE:** RUINS AT CHACO CANYON, NEW MEXICO

TREE RING DATING

One way that archaeologists are able to tell when a pueblo dwelling was built is by using a technique called "dendrochronology," or tree ring dating. Each year a tree grows a new ring of wood. Years with a lot of rainfall produce thick rings, while drier years produce thin rings. Trees of the same type growing in the same location have basically the same ring patterns. When a tree is cut down, we can count how many years ago it began to grow by counting the rings from the core of the tree outward to the trunk. Thus, we can assign a date to each tree ring beginning with the year it is cut down.

Because pueblo house beams were made from trees, they also have ring patterns on them. Archaeologists can tell what year a tree was cut down to use as a house beam by matching the tree ring pattern of the beam with the tree ring pattern of a newly cut tree. By determining the age of the beam, the archaeologists can determine when the house was constructed. They can also tell which years had a lot of rainfall and which were dry years by examining the thickness of the ring for any given year. This is how they were able to tell that there was a drought in the Southwest from A.D. 1276 to 1299.

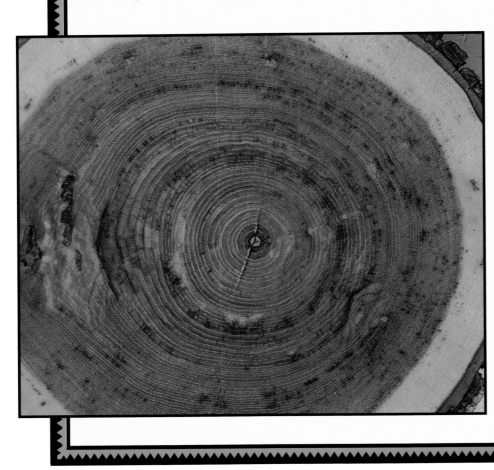

THE GROWTH RINGS OF A TREE ARE CLEARLY SEEN IN CROSS SECTION.

Influenced by the Hohokam and Mogollon, the Anasazi eventually began to farm and settle in permanent villages. At first they lived in circular pit houses, sometimes built in caves or rock overhangs. Each pit house sheltered an extended family, which might include a married couple and both their parents and their children. The pit houses were clustered in groups to form small villages, with between forty and 150 people living in each village.

Later (around A.D. 700), the Anasazi began to construct aboveground houses. The earliest aboveground dwellings were made by weaving branches through wooden supports. Then the walls were covered with mud, which would dry to a hard surface. From the time the Anasazi began to live above ground, they are known as Pueblos rather than Basket Makers. Between A.D. 1100 and 1300 the Anasazi established thriving communities centered in magnificent cities in various locations throughout the northern Southwest. They built towns in the sides of cliffs, beneath overhangs, and on top of mesas. They developed a complex social and religious system based on nature and the cycle of agriculture. They created beautiful pottery, weavings, turquoise jewelry, and clay figurines.

❧ **ABOVE**: FROG EFFIGY (OR FIGURINE), FROM PUEBLO BONITO, MADE OF JET AND INLAID TURQUOISE

❧ A Merging and Changing of Cultures

Since the Mogollon, Hohokam, and Anasazi all lived within several hundred miles, they often borrowed ideas from one another. Just as the Anasazi had been influenced by the Hohokam and Mogollon, these two cultures were later influenced by the Anasazi. Around A.D. 1100, the Mogollon and Hohokam began to build their homes above the ground. Anasazi influence among the Mogollon was very strong, and most archaeologists think that Mogollon culture eventually blended with Anasazi lifeways completely.

Among the Hohokam, artistic traditions began to change: the people eventually stopped making stone vessels, mirrors, clay figurines, and ball courts. Archaeologists believe that some sort of disaster, either environmental (such as floods or a change in climate) or cultural (such as strife within the group or a disruption in trade), forced the Hohokam to change their way of life drastically. In time, they abandoned their settlements altogether. Most archaeologists think that the Hohokam remained in the area, giving rise to some of the Native American peoples living in the Southwest today. A small number of archaeologists argue that the Hohokam migrated out of the area entirely.

The Anasazi, at that point the largest and most highly organized civilization in the Southwest, had reached a peak in their technological and cultural development.

🔥 Living in a Cliff Dwelling

By building their cities in cliffs and on mesas, the Anasazi were more protected from attacking enemies than they would have been on lower ground. Their buildings were made of rooms clustered together and could be as high as four or five stories. On the ground level the structures could be six or eight rooms deep. The pit

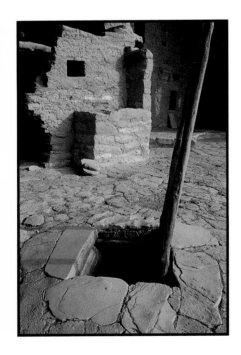

houses once used by the Anasazi became sacred areas of ritual activity, called "kivas," and were entered by ladders leading from ground level down. In the larger towns, the houses, storage rooms, kivas, and plazas were usually arranged so that the town was built in a D shape. Outside the towns were fields

🔥 **ABOVE**: THIS BUILDING AT MESA VERDE NATIONAL PARK IS KNOWN AS SPRUCE TREE HOUSE. IN THE FOREGROUND, A LADDER LEADS DOWN INTO A KIVA.
RIGHT: A VIEW OF PUEBLO BONITO WITH KIVAS IN THE FOREGROUND

ACOMA PUEBLO AND THE ENCHANTED MESA

In the midst of a wide expanse of grassy valley in New Mexico, a sandstone mesa stands apart from other surrounding land formations. The mesa is steep-sided and rises over 350 feet (107m) upward. On its flat top is the town of Acoma, one of the most picturesque pueblos in the Southwest and one of the oldest continually inhabited communities in North America.

The first Europeans to see Acoma Pueblo were sixteenth-century Spanish explorers. As they approached the pueblo, traveling across the valley, they could hardly distinguish the rectangular buildings above them that blended so well into the surrounding rock. To reach the city, they had to climb a single, hand-built stairway carved into the rock along one side of the mesa. Later, Acoma would be called "Sky City" by tourists because of its location high above the valley floor.

A few miles east of Acoma, another mesa stands more than four hundred feet (122m) above the valley. This mesa is called "Kadzima" in the Keresan language (the language of the Acoma people). Because it is so awe-inspiring, outsiders have given it the name "Enchanted Mesa." According to the Acoma people, Enchanted Mesa was home to their ancestors.

◖ ACOMA PUEBLO, KNOWN TO TOURISTS AS "SKY CITY"

of corn, beans, and squash irrigated by a network of ditches and dams made of earth and stone.

One of the most spectacular areas of Anasazi development was in Chaco Canyon, located in present-day New Mexico. From about A.D. 900 to 1200, Chaco Canyon was a hub of urban activity supporting roughly six thousand people. Eight major pueblos were built within a nine-mile (14½km) stretch in the canyon. These were linked to one another and to smaller towns (some as far as a hundred miles [160km] from the canyon) by a network of roads. To build the towns, workers had to travel, sometimes as far as thirty miles (48km), to bring back timber and other building materials.

The largest town in Chaco Canyon is called Pueblo Bonito (which means "Beautiful Town"). Pueblo Bonito had over eight hundred rooms and probably had about one thousand people living there. There were no doors

KOKOPELLI

One of the most popular figures in rock art is the flute player, called "Kokopelli" by the Hopi. The earliest flute players are found in Anasazi rock art, and some of the images are nearly two thousand years old. Kokopelli is a fertility symbol, and he is often shown courting the rain that will ensure good crops. In the hump on his back he is said to carry presents for young maidens. Kokopelli is still depicted by the Pueblos, and you can find him on T-shirts and charm bracelets, as well as in ancient rock art.

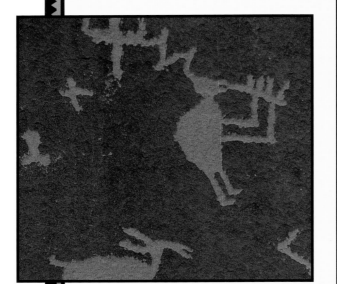

🌿 ANASAZI PETROGLYPH DEPICTING THE FLUTE PLAYER, FROM VILLAGE OF THE GREAT KIVAS IN ZUNI-CIBOLA NATIONAL PARK, NEW MEXICO

or windows on the outside walls. This was typical of the larger towns. To enter, a person had to climb a ladder over the wall. Pueblo Bonito had two Great Kivas, forty feet (12m) and sixty feet (18½m) wide, in addition to several smaller ones used by families. In these kivas the people performed sacred rituals probably not very different from those performed by Pueblo peoples today.

dwellings at Mesa Verde is Cliff Palace, a complex of more than two hundred rooms and twenty-three kivas. To reach the dwellings, the people had to climb the cliff face using hand- and footholds. To reach the different levels of rooms within the settlement, ladders were used.

Today places like Chaco Canyon and Mesa Verde stand as proof of the Anasazi people's achievements in engineering. They also tell us that the Anasazi functioned as a well-organized,

Another important center of Anasazi life was the site now known as Mesa Verde, located in Colorado. The people of Mesa Verde began their settlement in about A.D. 550, building their homes on the mesa top. Around 1190 they began to build their dwellings in natural curves in the cliffsides, but they continued to plant their fields above on the flat mesa. One of the grandest cliff

cooperative society. If they did not cooperate with one another, they could not have succeeded in developing such elaborate towns and irrigation networks. Furthermore, Anasazi civilization was built without benefit of metal tools, plows, horses, oxen, or other pack animals. Farming and building were successfully done using creativity and physical strength.

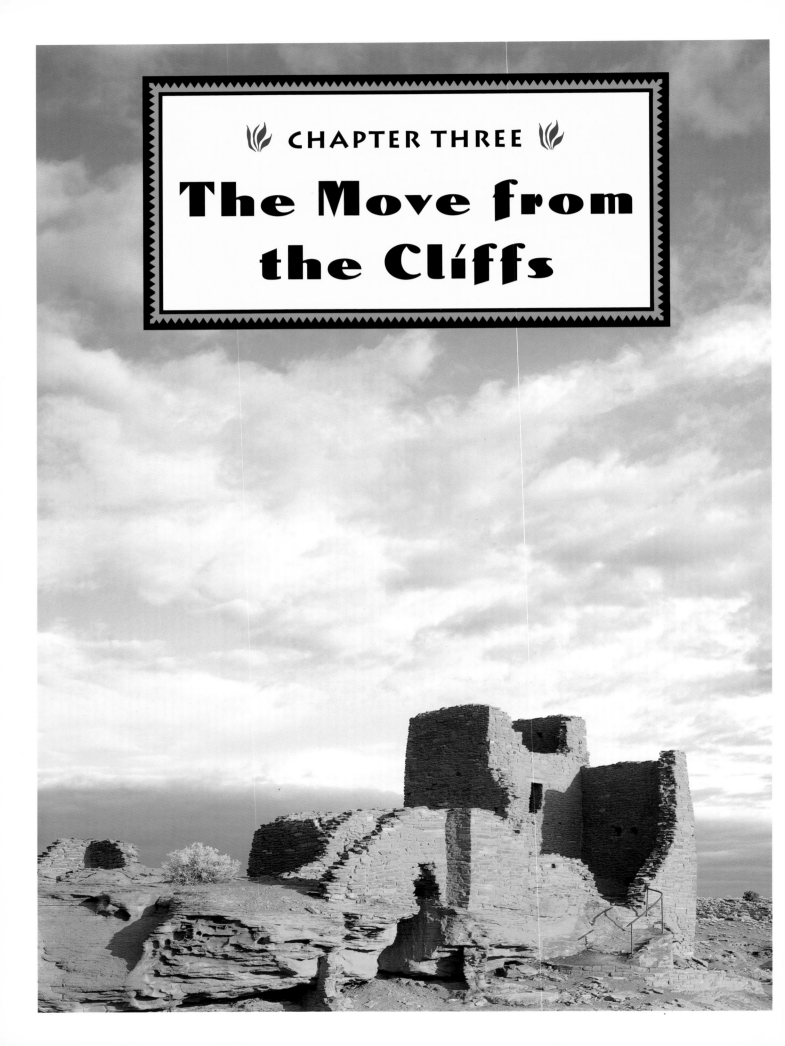

CHAPTER THREE

The Move from the Cliffs

🌿 The Move

By A.D. 1300 the Anasazi began to abandon their cities. No one knows for sure why this happened, but archaeologists have various explanations. Perhaps, in spite of their good defenses, the Anasazi were run off the land by attacking enemies. Perhaps an epidemic spread through the area, killing much of the population and causing the survivors to flee to an area that was free of disease. Some say the Anasazi overused their natural resources, especially the timber that they used to build the beams of their dwellings. Also, erosion of the land and changes in weather patterns probably made farming more difficult.

Most likely, the Anasazi left because of a combination of factors, including severe droughts in the area spanning twenty-three years, from 1276 to 1299. These harsh conditions may have caused so much stress among the people that they began to fight among themselves and were no longer able to have the cooperative relations necessary for the cities to function. Whatever the reasons, the Anasazi left the cities they had lived in for centuries and spread out, searching for new lands to farm. Eventually they spread southward, founding the pueblos encountered by the Spanish in the sixteenth century.

🌿 Plazas and Buildings

When the Anasazi moved they took their customs with them, and wherever they settled they continued to build pueblos. In the west, pueblos were built of sandstone, a fine-grained rock that looks like tightly packed grains of sand. Sandstone is abundant in the area of the western pueblos and was cut into building blocks. Along the river, buildings were made of adobe, a kind of natural

🌿 **OPPOSITE**: ANASAZI RUINS AGAINST A DRAMATIC SKY. **ABOVE**: ZUNI PUEBLO IN EARLY TIMES AFTER THE ARRIVAL OF THE SPANISH

clay found nearby. It is sticky when wet, but dries hard. Because of this quality, adobe was used in all the pueblos as mortar and plaster.

Each pueblo house consisted of one large, rectangular room. Rooms were added whenever a new home was necessary. By adding homes when needed, pueblo dwellings took on the look of many boxes placed one on top of another in a terraced formation. These clustered dwellings were built around a plaza, or square, at the center of the town. Other buildings included underground ceremonial kivas and storehouses.

🌿 PLASTERING AN ADOBE WALL

The first step in making a pueblo dwelling was to build the walls. Depending on the area, the walls of pueblo buildings were constructed using one of two methods. The western Pueblo peoples cut sandstone into blocks and stacked them as building stones in masonry construction. The blocks were laid one atop another like bricks, using adobe as mortar, until a wall was completed. Chinks between the building stones were filled in with smaller rocks. The roof was made by crossing the main beams with a series of smaller poles placed close together, producing a crosshatched effect. Layers of branches, grasses, twigs, and brush were placed over this, and finally a layer of mud was laid down and packed hard.

The eastern Pueblo peoples used only adobe. Sometimes they mixed the adobe with ash, formed the mixture into balls of clay, and used these balls as building stones, much like the western Pueblos used sandstone blocks. Another method was to build up the walls in sections. As each section was made, adobe was placed between two rectangular frames to keep its form until the clay dried. The frames were then removed and placed beside the newly completed section of wall. Then the builder repeated the process until an entire wall was finished. Sometimes, instead of using the frames, builders would mix the adobe with small stones, when available, and the mixture would be thick enough to stand on its own as it dried. After the walls were finished, timbers were laid across the top of the building to support the roof, which was flat and could be used as an open terrace for sitting or working. Because the workers had only stone tools and cutting timber was a hard job, the workers let the ends of the timbers stick out of the completed roof. When the walls and roof were finished, the entire dwelling was usually plastered with adobe. The average pueblo dwelling was about seven or eight feet (2 or 2½m) high,

twelve feet (3½m) wide, and twenty feet (6m) long. Although the materials used to make these dwellings were strong, erosion from wind and rain made it necessary to repair them periodically.

Each pueblo dwelling had only a few small windows. There were no doors on the ground floor; to get into a first-floor dwelling, a person had to climb a ladder and enter through an opening in the roof. In case of attack by raiding enemies, the ladders could be pulled up onto the roofs so the enemy could not follow. Pueblo dwellings were designed for maximum protection from enemies and for the comfort of the persons living in them. The thick walls and roofs absorbed heat during the day and released it at night, so the dwellings remained relatively cool during the hot days and warm during the cold nights.

Pueblo peoples whitewashed the interior walls of their dwellings using gypsum, a mineral found in the

A FAMILY RELAXES AT HOME IN THIS SCENE OF EARLY PUEBLO LIFE.

🌿 INSIDE AN ADOBE DWELLING IN EARLY TIMES

area. The gypsum was dissolved in water and then washed over the walls with a piece of animal skin. They built storage shelves into the walls and a fireplace into a corner of the room. Cooking utensils were kept beside the fireplace, including a large cooking pot, gourd containers and dippers, and a broom made of grass for sweeping the hearth and floor.

Another important feature of the pueblo dwelling was the set of metates, or milling stones, used to grind corn. Usually there were three metates arranged inside a wooden frame, and each metate had its own compart-ment within the frame. The metates, made of different kinds of rock, were of three textures. The worker, using a stone cylinder called a "mano," would first grind the corn on the metate of the roughest texture. Then the corn was ground further on a metate of less rough texture, and finally it was ground smooth on the metate with the finest texture to make the corn into a fine flour.

There were no cabinets, tables, or chairs in the pueblo dwelling. Clothing and blankets were hung either from the roof beams sticking out of the walls or on a pole attached to the beams. Bowls and other items were stored in niches in the walls. People ate, slept, and worked sitting on the floor, often on blankets or rugs.

Both men and women worked together to build pueblo dwellings. The men hauled building materials, built the walls, and put the roof timbers in place. The women worked on the roofs, covered the building with adobe, and whitewashed the interiors. Often, when a couple needed to build their own home, friends and relatives helped them. In most pueblos, when the home was completed, it belonged to the woman of the household.

This spirit of cooperation was evident not only in house building, but in the way the pueblo community was run. Almost all activities within the pueblo, including work, play, and religious ceremonies, were communal activities. There was no single leader who ruled the pueblo at any one time. Rather, each community had certain religious groups whose members would decide on important issues concerning the pueblo. The religious groups also had their own priesthoods. Members of a priesthood sat on the town council, which was responsible for pueblo policies and lawmaking. Those individuals who attained leadership roles were persons who used their wisdom and knowledge to guide the people in important decision making.

Although the various Pueblo peoples had many customs in common, each pueblo was an independent town that functioned on its own. Pueblos traded with one another and with other Native American groups, but they were not dependent on this trade to live. Rather, the people within each community worked together to make sure they had all the things necessary for survival in their harsh environment.

DRIED CORN WAS STORED IN POTTERY AND GROUND INTO CORNMEAL AND FLOUR USING THE STONE MANO AND METATE.

CHAPTER FOUR
Daily Life

Farming the Desert

The dry desert environment made growing crops a difficult task. The Pueblo peoples used all water sources available to them and never wasted this important life-giving element. River pueblo dwellers had the Rio Grande to help them water their crops, but desert pueblo dwellers did not have a nearby water source. Rainwater was important for all the Pueblo peoples and was captured in reservoirs made of rock. Snow was gathered into tremendous snowballs and also put in the reservoirs to melt. To regulate the flow of water into the fields, the people dug irrigation ditches and built dams out of earth and brush.

Farming took careful planning. The farmers had to figure out the best place to plant to maximize the water supply. They determined where sources of underground water were, and in these areas they planted their crops deep in the ground so that the roots could reach to this natural source of water. About twenty seeds were planted in each deep hole the farmer made in the hope that some would grow.

The main crops of corn and squash were planted in large fields outside the pueblo. Sometimes they were planted miles away and families would move to them, setting up

AN ANCIENT AMERICAN CROP

Corn, or maize, the Pueblo peoples' most important crop, is a plant that is native to the Americas. Corn was being cultivated by Native peoples in Mexico at least six thousand years ago. This practice then eventually spread both northward and southward, and corn became a staple crop for Native Americans throughout the Western Hemisphere. Over the centuries, hundreds of varieties were grown in various shapes, sizes, and colors such as red, blue, and yellow.

SOME OF THE MANY VARIETIES OF CORN, BEANS, AND CHILI PEPPERS GROWN BY PUEBLO FARMERS

OPPOSITE: EARLY PUEBLO FARMERS KEEPING WATCH OVER THEIR FIELDS

temporary shelters, during the planting and harvesting seasons. Other fields were not as far, and families would tend them daily.

In addition to the main fields, all families planted smaller gardens closer to their homes. Here they grew crops such as beans, chili peppers, and cotton. These smaller crops were usually grown close to a water source, often a spring, and were watered by hand during dry spells. The gardens were made by forming low ridges into squares, each square surrounding a plant, in a waffle pattern. Today they are known as waffle gardens. The ridges of earth helped to hold the water around the plant. To keep out animals, waffle gardens were usually surrounded by low adobe walls.

To ensure that they had a food supply in times of drought, the Pueblo peoples preserved and stored much of their crop yields. At harvest time, after the crops were picked, the vegetables were laid out on roofs or hung from beams and poles to dry. This would preserve the food for later use. The preserved food was stored in the inner rooms of dwelling clusters.

In addition to vegetable foods, which made up most of the Pueblo diet, they sometimes ate meat. Deer and antelope were hunted by organized parties of men who drove the animals into pitfalls or other traps. Smaller animals, such as rabbits, squirrels, and fox, were also hunted for food. Besides meat, the larger animals provided skins, sinew for sewing and making bowstrings, and bones for fashioning tools. In addition to the foods they grew, the Pueblo peoples also ate roots, berries, piñon nuts, and other wild plant foods.

PUEBLO PEOPLES FARMING THE DESERT. BECAUSE CROPS LIKE MAIZE COULD BE PRESERVED AND STORED, THEY PROVIDED A BACKUP FOOD SUPPLY FOR TIMES WHEN WILD PLANTS WERE SCARCE.

The Pueblo Family

The Pueblo family was matrilineal, that is, each person traced descent through his or her mother's side of the family. A Pueblo child, therefore, belonged to his mother's clan, and when a man married he moved into the home of his wife's family.

Traditionally, the Pueblo man wore a shirt, breechclout (or loincloth), and kilt of soft deerskin or woven cotton, with leather moccasins or sandals made of woven yucca fiber on his feet. A woman wore a garment of woven cotton in the shape of a large rectangle that was wrapped around the body and fastened on the right

THE SHUTTLECOCK GAME

One game enjoyed by Pueblo children was shuttlecock. (A shuttlecock is a light object, usually with feathers attached to it, that is hit with the hand or a paddle.) Pueblo peoples often made shuttlecocks by folding cornhusks and then attaching feathers to the cornhusk packet. Using one hand, the shuttlecock was hit upward with the palm. A player was supposed to hit the shuttlecock without missing for a certain number of throws, and opposing players would wage bets against one another.

A HOPI CHILD TODAY WEARING THE TRADITIONAL "SQUASH BLOSSOM" HAIRSTYLE OF UNMARRIED GIRLS

shoulder. A wide cloth belt was then wrapped several times around the waist. Women often went barefoot, but sometimes they wore high boots of deerskin; these boots were moccasin-style, with strips of deerskin that were wrapped several times around their legs.

Both men and women usually wore their long hair braided, doubled over, and fastened at the back of the neck with bangs in the front. Among the Hopi, unmarried girls wore their hair in the "squash blossom" style—large whorls on either side of the head, held in place by a frame made of cornhusk or other plant fiber.

LEARNING FROM POTSHERDS

Pueblo peoples, like peoples all over the world, have long used natural clays to make pottery for cooking, storage, and, in modern times, art objects. After a piece of pottery was formed, it

was baked in an outdoor kiln so that the clay could harden. The pottery was then often painted with designs and figures using natural paints of crushed mineral pigments and brushes made of chewed yucca leaves.

This pottery is found in abundance at ancient southwestern sites. Sometimes the pottery is broken into pieces called "sherds." Each southwestern culture had its own way of making and decorating its pottery. Over time, and in different locations, pottery styles and methods of making the pottery have changed. By analyzing the pots or potsherds, archaeologists are able to tell when and by what culture the pottery was produced.

The early Anasazi typically used a black-on-white color scheme for their pottery, while the Mogollon tended to favor a brown-on-red combination. When the two cultures merged, artisans formed a new tradition using brown, black, white, and red. Much of the Pueblo pottery that is produced today is still decorated with these traditional colors.

LEFT: POTSHERDS FROM CHACO CANYON, NEW MEXICO. **BELOW:** TO MAKE POTTERY HARD AND DURABLE, IT IS FIRED IN A CLAY OVEN, OR KILN.

STORYTELLER DOLLS

For centuries the Pueblo peoples have been making clay figurines in human form. But it was not until 1964 that clay storyteller dolls were first made by Helen Cordero, an artist from Cochiti Pueblo. Although storyteller dolls are a modern creation, these figures honor the ancient tradition of storytelling and serve as a reminder of the important role storytellers have always had in Pueblo life.

ABOVE: CLAY STORYTELLER DOLLS ARE ALWAYS ADORNED WITH SMALLER FIGURES REPRESENTING THE CHILDREN WHO GATHER AROUND TO LISTEN TO THE STORIES.

Each dawn the Pueblo community began its day. Men and boys headed for the fields, while women and girls worked to prepare the day's meals. By helping the adults, children learned the practical skills they would need to know as adults. Young boys started out clearing brush from the fields and scaring away birds that had come to eat the seeds. When they grew older, boys would help with the heavier work of farming. Back at the pueblo, girls helped to grind corn on the metates, cook, and bake bread in the family's outdoor clay ovens.

Children also learned artistic traditions from their elders. Boys, for example, learned how to weave from their male relatives, while girls learned how to make pottery from their female relatives.

In the late afternoon, the men and boys returned from the fields and every family sat down for a meal. In

EARLY PUEBLO WOMEN, HELPED BY THEIR DAUGHTERS AND NIECES, FETCH WATER FROM A RIVER.

Pueblo women preparing corn. The young woman in the foreground removes the dried kernels from the cob, while the women in the background grind the kernels using a set of metates, or milling stones.

the evening, families would visit one another. The children would play and the adults would talk and enjoy each other's company before nightfall, when everyone would go to bed.

During the winter, when the men were not involved in planting or harvesting, they would spend their time making tools and weaving. Winter was also the special time for storytelling, when children would gather around and listen to the tales of the elders. These stories taught children lessons about life and the Pueblo peoples' history and spiritual traditions. These stories were entertaining to children and adults alike. In addition to listening to stories, children and adults played games, including racing games and guessing games, like the hidden ball game in which a person had to guess under which wooden cylinder a pebble or bean was hidden. Much of the Pueblo person's time was also spent preparing for the many rituals and ceremonies that were so essential to their daily lives.

PIKI

The Pueblo peoples sometimes built small rooms in which a certain type of bread, called "piki," was made. Piki required a special stove, made of a stone slab held up by other stone slabs, forming a small table; a fire was built underneath. Preparing the stove for use took a long time. It had to be heated slowly so that the stone would not crack, and the surface had to be treated with oil and piñon gum. Once the stove was ready, a Pueblo woman, using only her hands, carefully and skillfully covered its surface with a thin layer of batter made from blue cornmeal. The finished bread was tissue-paper thin and rolled like parchment. It was eaten at regular meals and given to dancers during ceremonies. Piki is still made today by the Pueblo peoples in the traditional manner.

Making piki bread

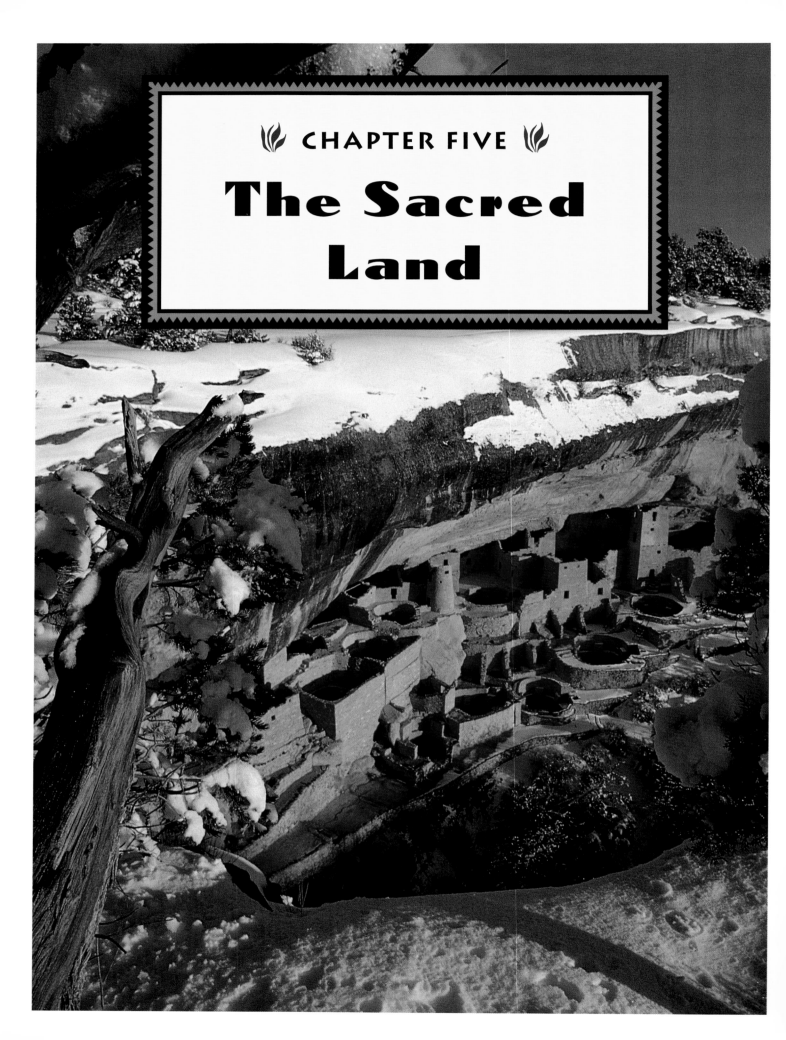

CHAPTER FIVE
The Sacred Land

The Supernatural World

Spirituality was at the heart of Pueblo life. Just about everything a person did was connected to his or her spiritual beliefs, and prayers of thanksgiving and requests for blessings were recited at almost all activities, both personal and communal. To the Pueblo, all life was connected and the land itself was a sacred place. Each natural thing, from rocks to humans, had a life force and a particular character. Because of these beliefs, the Pueblo person felt at one with all around him or her; the individual was a part of the wholeness of the universe.

According to Pueblo belief, certain natural forces were manifested in spirits and supernatural beings that lived underground, in the sky, and in the four directions of the world. These included animal spirits, friendly spirits called "kachinas," war gods, spirits of the Pueblos' ancestors, and others. These beings were powerful, and so they were called upon to help the people in various ways, especially in helping to keep the crops growing and the game animals abundant.

From this sincere belief in the power of supernatural beings, the Pueblo peoples developed a complex series of rituals and ceremonies that centered around agriculture and the need for rain in the dry environment in which they lived. The ceremonial cycle coincided with the different stages of agriculture. There were ceremonies in spring for planting and growth, and in the summer ceremonies asking for rain and protection for the crops were held. Ceremonies of thanksgiving and prayers for a good crop in the following year were held during harvest time in the autumn. In winter, ceremonies centered around asking for successful hunts, for water in the form of snow, and for protection against freezing blizzards and winds.

OPPOSITE: Cliff Palace in winter. **Above**: This mural, painted on a kiva wall, dates to about a.d. 1500.

The Kiva

Pueblo peoples believed that life began underground in a place known as the First World. Over time, people emerged onto a second, higher level below the earth, called the Second World, which was closer to the surface of the ground. Then they continued onto a third level, higher still, known as the Third World. Finally, the people emerged aboveground into the world we know today, called the Fourth World. Those who emerged were the ancestors of the Pueblo peoples, and they danced in celebration of the good new world they had found.

🌿 **LEFT**: AT PECOS NATIONAL MONUMENT, THE RUINS OF AN EARLY SPANISH MISSION STAND BEHIND THE RUINS OF A KIVA. **ABOVE**: SPECTATORS WATCH FROM THE ROOFTOPS AS MASKED KACHINA DANCERS ARRIVE IN PROCESSION FOR A CEREMONY.

The kiva, the Pueblo ceremonial chamber, was symbolic of this underworld. The kiva was a circular room that was usually built underground. Kivas were entered by climbing down a ladder that led from a hole in the roof. Every kiva's floor had a hole that was overlaid with a piece of wood. This cavity represented the place from which the Pueblos' ancestors emerged from the lower worlds and through which the prayers of the people reached the supernatural beings who still lived below.

The kiva was central to the religious life of the community, for it was there that Pueblo men stored their ritual objects and met to plan and perform the sacred

KACHINAS

Kachinas are supernatural beings that bring blessing to the people and rain for the crops. They are honored at ceremonies given throughout six months of each year. The word kachina can mean three things: the actual supernatural being, a ceremonial dancer dressed as one of the kachinas, or a carved figure of a kachina made from the root of a cottonwood tree. There are hundreds of different kachinas. Some of them are listed here using their Hopi names.

Tocha (Hummingbird Kachina)

Koyemsi (Mudhead Clown Kachina)

Qocha Mana (White Corn Maiden Kachina)

Tawa (Sun Kachina)

Nata-aska (Black Ogre Kachina)

Talavai (Early Morning Kachina)

Mongwa (Great Horned Owl Kachina)

Sowi'ing (Deer Kachina)

Polik Mana (Butterfly Maiden Kachina)

Kwa (Eagle Kachina)

ABOVE LEFT: KANA-A (SUNSET CRATER KACHINA). **ABOVE RIGHT**: KWASA-ITAKA (DRESS KACHINA). **LEFT**: HO-OTE, A GUARD KACHINA

rituals essential to the community's well-being. These rituals were performed by various religious groups, or societies, each of which had its own special role in carrying out the highly organized set of practices associated with each ceremony. The kiva was a men's house in which women and children were generally not allowed. Men's exclusive role in religion helped to balance the power that women held in the Pueblo peoples' matrilineal society.

Each Pueblo man belonged to a religious society. Boys were initiated into societies in a series of stages. They were brought into the kiva and introduced to masked figures claiming to be the kachinas. They would later find that the kachinas were men of the pueblo who, when dressed as the kachinas for ceremony, took

on the kachinas' spiritual power. With further instruction, the boys learned the rituals, obligations, and secrets of the societies. Eventually, they would be old enough to become adult members of the group and participate as masked dancers themselves.

Sacred rituals in the kiva were secret and well guarded from outsiders. Public ceremonies held in the town plaza usually began with private rituals in the kiva, where men fasted, prayed, purified themselves, and made offerings to the supernaturals of cornmeal, corn pollen, and prayer sticks (feathered sticks painted with sacred symbols). After a great deal of preparation in the kivas, dancers emerged in bright costumes and body paint symbolizing many elements from Pueblo spiritual beliefs.

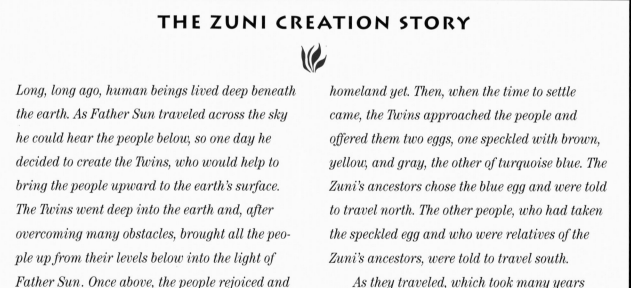

THE ZUNI CREATION STORY

Long, long ago, human beings lived deep beneath the earth. As Father Sun traveled across the sky he could hear the people below, so one day he decided to create the Twins, who would help to bring the people upward to the earth's surface. The Twins went deep into the earth and, after overcoming many obstacles, brought all the people up from their levels below into the light of Father Sun. Once above, the people rejoiced and began the long journey to find the place where they would make their home.

The people traveled together, stopping and settling at different places over the years, although they knew they had not found the

homeland yet. Then, when the time to settle came, the Twins approached the people and offered them two eggs, one speckled with brown, yellow, and gray, the other of turquoise blue. The Zuni's ancestors chose the blue egg and were told to travel north. The other people, who had taken the speckled egg and who were relatives of the Zuni's ancestors, were told to travel south.

As they traveled, which took many years more, they developed their religious societies and ceremonies. Finally, they found the homeland and settled. Today, the places the ancestors traveled through are still remembered and are sacred places for the modern Zuni.

❧ CONCLUSION ❧
Modern Pueblo Life

In 1540 the Pueblo peoples made their first contact with Europeans. At that time, members of an expedition led by the Spanish explorer Francisco Vásquez de Coronado entered the region from Mexico looking for a legendary place called the Seven Cities of Cibola. Later, in 1598, the Spanish began colonizing the area. Because their methods of converting the Pueblo peoples to Christianity were often harsh, in 1680 the various pueblos united in revolt against the Spanish. The revolt succeeded for a time, but the Spanish returned in 1692 and once again established rule over the area.

❧ SHEEP GRAZE IN THE VALLEY NEAR ACOMA PUEBLO, WHICH WAS FIRST VISITED BY THE SPANISH IN 1541.

The Spanish were followed by other non-Pueblo peoples moving into the Southwest. With new people came new ideas, and the Pueblo peoples were able to adapt these new ideas to their own lifestyle. New crops, like wheat and onions, were added to the Pueblo mainstays of corn, beans, and squash. Sheep, brought over by the Spanish, were sometimes used for their wool, which the Pueblo peoples began to weave in addition to cotton. When the railroad came through the Southwest in the late 1800s, new products including cloth and utensils were obtained and used.

PRESERVING THE PAST

ings underneath the canyon wall. They had accidently come upon Cliff Palace, the largest complex in Mesa Verde.

Over the years the Wetherills explored the area, finding more ruins and many artifacts. They advertised their finds and attracted tourists to the ruins. They charged for guided tours and rented rooms on their ranch to visitors. As visitors came and went, they often took souvenirs like pottery and tools with them. (This was before laws were passed that protected sites like Mesa Verde.) Fearing that the site would be completely pillaged, McClurg and Peabody pushed their campaign for its protection. They won in 1906 when President Theodore Roosevelt made Mesa Verde a national park.

The first national park dedicated to preserving ancient American culture was Mesa Verde. This was the result of the efforts of two concerned citizens, Virginia McClurg and Lucy Peabody, who worried that the unprotected ruins were being damaged by visitors.

The ruins of Mesa Verde were first introduced to the public by a family named Wetherill. In 1888, Richard Wetherill and his brother-in-law Charles Mason were out riding on Mesa Verde. As they came to the edge of a canyon, they looked across and saw a spectacular ruin of stone build-

❧ **ABOVE LEFT:** THE RUINS OF CLIFF PALACE AT MESA VERDE NATIONAL PARK. WHILE YELLOWSTONE WAS THE FIRST NATIONAL PARK EVER ESTABLISHED IN THE UNITED STATES, MESA VERDE WAS THE FIRST NATIONAL PARK ESTABLISHED FOR THE PURPOSE OF PRESERVING ANCIENT NATIVE AMERICAN CULTURE. **ABOVE RIGHT:** PAINTINGS ADORN THE WALLS OF THE TOWER AT CLIFF PALACE.

Not all outside influence was beneficial to the Pueblo peoples. Government boarding schools, for example, were established, which required Pueblo children to leave their homes and learn Christianity and the ways of mainstream America. Yet in spite of all the changes that have taken place throughout history, Pueblo peoples have managed to maintain their ancient traditions to a great degree. While Pueblo peoples today make livings in various occupations, some in cities far from the pueblo, many continue the ancient tradition of farming and relying on the land. In addition, many supplement their incomes as artists and craftspeople, making drums, jewelry, and the magnificent pottery for which the Pueblo peoples are famous.

Although most pueblo dwellings today are built using cinderblocks, lumber, and other store-bought materials, the Pueblo community is still built with the same principles in mind. The kiva continues to be an important feature in modern pueblos, and the year-round ceremonies that are

🌿 A YOUNG CEREMONIAL DANCER DRESSED IN A COW HIDE AT SAN JUAN PUEBLO

🌿 THE FAMOUS SAN ILDEFONSO POTTER JULIAN MARTINEZ AT WORK. IN 1919, JULIAN AND HIS WIFE, MARIA, WERE THE FIRST TO DEVELOP THE TECHNIQUE OF MAKING BLACK-ON-BLACK POTTERY.

at the heart of Pueblo spiritual traditions still play a vital role in the lives of the people.

When the Spanish first arrived in the sixteenth century there were about eighty-five pueblos in the Southwest. Today there are nineteen in New Mexico and, in Arizona, several villages of the Hopi. Each pueblo is run under its own leadership system. United in tradition, the Pueblo peoples of today continue to recognize the importance of the ancient ways of their ancestors.

World Time Line

1000–500 B.C.   **Southwest:**
Agriculture begins.

The World:
Olmec civilization is under way in Mexico; King David rules the Israelites in the Middle East; Taoism develops in China.

500 B.C.–A.D. 1   **Southwest:**
Mogollon culture emerges (300 B.C.); pottery techniques are developed (100 B.C.); Hohokam culture emerges (A.D. 1).

The World:
Buddhism develops in Asia; Greek and Roman cultures flourish; Cleopatra rules Egypt.

A.D. 1–900   **Southwest:**
The Anasazi are in their Basket Maker period (A.D. 1–400).

The World:
Christianity and Islam develop in the Middle East; Maya civilization flourishes in Mexico; the Roman city of Pompeii is destroyed (A.D. 79); a "Golden Age" flourishes in China under the Tang Dynasty (A.D. 618–907); the empire of Ghana flourishes in Africa.

A.D. 900–1300   **Southwest:**
Chaco Canyon cities flourish (A.D. 900–1200); Anasazi culture reaches its technological peak (A.D. 1100–1300); Mesa Verde inhabitants move from mesa tops to cliffsides (A.D. 1190); severe drought makes farming difficult (A.D. 1276–1299).

The World:
The Mongols invade China under the leadership of Genghis Khan (1210); Marco Polo sets out to explore Asia (1271); the Crusades (Holy Wars) are under way in Europe and the Middle East; the empire of Mali flourishes in Africa; the age of the samurai warriors is under way in Japan.

A.D. 1300–1600   **Southwest:**
The Anasazi begin to abandon their cities (A.D. 1300); Pueblo peoples have first contact with Europeans (A.D. 1540).

The World:
Inca civilization flourishes in South America; Aztec civilization flourishes in Mexico; the Renaissance is under way in Europe; Timbuktu flourishes as a center of commerce and Muslim culture in Africa.

❧ Glossary

adobe A natural clay used by some Pueblo peoples to build their dwellings.

Anasazi Ancestors of the present-day Pueblo peoples who lived in the canyons and mesas of the Four Corners region of the Southwest from approximately A.D. 200 to 1450.

Basket Makers A name given to the Anazasi to mark the period from about A.D. 1 to 400, when they did fine basketry work but did not yet make pottery.

Chaco Canyon An Anasazi site in New Mexico that flourished between A.D. 900 and 1200.

Cliff Dwellers A name given to the Anasazi because of their custom of building their homes in cliffs and over-hangs and on mesas.

Cliff Palace A magnificent cliff dwelling at Mesa Verde with two hundred rooms and twenty-three kivas.

dendrochronology A dating technique used by archaeologists based on analyzing tree rings.

desert pueblos Pueblos built west of the Rio Grande.

Hohokam Ancient peoples of the Southwest who lived in the desert region of southern Arizona from approximately A.D. 200 to 1450.

kachina A Pueblo supernatural being, a masked dancer representing the supernatural being, or a carved figure of the supernatural being.

kiva A circular room used by Pueblo peoples for rituals.

lifeway The traditions, customs, and daily practices of a people.

matrilineal A system whereby a person traces his or her descent through the mother's side of the family.

mesa   A land formation with a flat top and steep sides.

Mesa Verde   An Anasazi site in Colorado at which the Anasazi first built their dwellings on the mesa top and then abandoned them to build new dwellings in the sides of cliffs.

metate   A stone used to grind corn and other foods.

Mimbres   A branch of the Mogollon known for their black-on-white painted pottery.

Mogollon   Ancestors of the present-day Pueblo peoples who lived from approximately A.D. 200 to 1450 in the mountainous area ranging from the borders of Arizona and New Mexico into northern Mexico.

petroglyph   A carving chiseled into the surface of a rock or canyon wall.

piñon   A type of pine tree with edible seeds that grows in the Southwest.

pit house   A style of house, usually round, partially dug into the ground and covered with a framework of wood, brush, and earth.

plateau   A flat area of land that is raised above the surrounding land on at least one side.

prayer stick   A feathered stick painted with sacred symbols and used as an offering to the supernaturals in Pueblo rituals.

Pueblo Bonito   The largest pueblo at Chaco Canyon.

river pueblos   Pueblos built along the Rio Grande.

waffle garden   A small garden made by forming low ridges into squares, each square surrounding a plant, in a waffle pattern.

🔥 Bibliography

Coe, Michael, Dean Snow, and Elizabeth Benson. *Atlas of Ancient America.* New York: Facts on File, 1989.

Elder, John, and Hertha D. Wong, eds. *Family of Earth and Sky: Indigenous Tales of Nature from Around the World.* Boston: Beacon Press, 1994.

Griffin-Pierce, Trudy. *The Encyclopedia of Native America.* New York: Viking, 1995.

Hirschfelder, Arlene, and Martha Kreipe de Montano. *The Native American Almanac: A Portrait of Native America Today.* New York: Prentice Hall, 1993.

Josephy, Alvin M., Jr. *The Indian Heritage of America.* New York: Alfred A. Knopf, 1985.

Kopper, Philip. *The Smithsonian Book of North American Indians: Before the Coming of the Europeans.* Washington, D.C.: Smithsonian Books, 1986.

Mays, Buddy. *Ancient Cities of the Southwest: A Practical Guide to the Major Prehistoric Ruins of Arizona, New Mexico, Utah, and Colorado.* San Francisco: Chronicle Books, 1990.

———. *Indian Villages of the Southwest: A Practical Guide to the Pueblo Indian Villages of New Mexico and Arizona.* San Francisco: Chronicle Books, 1985.

Sherman, Josepha. *Indian Tribes of North America.* New York: Portland House, 1990.

Snow, Dean. *The Archaeology of North America.* New York: The Viking Press, 1976.

Sturtevant, William C., gen. ed., and Alfonso Ortiz, vol. ed. *Handbook of North American Indians: Southwest.* Volume 9. Washington, D.C.: Smithsonian Institution, 1979.

Thomas, David Hurst. *Exploring Ancient Native America: An Archaeological Guide.* New York: Macmillan, 1994.

Time-Life editors. *Mound Builders and Cliff Dwellers.* Lost Civilizations series. Alexandria, Va.: Time-Life Books, 1992.

Trimble, Stephen. *The People: Indians of the American Southwest.* Santa Fe: School of American Research Press, 1993.

Wright, Barton. *Hopi Kachinas: The Complete Guide to Collecting Kachina Dolls.* Northland Publishing, 1988.

Index

Page numbers in *italics* refer to photographs and illustrations.

Photo-graphy Credits